Alongside

Also by Anne Compton

Alongside

Anne Compton

Fitzhenry & Whiteside

Published in Canada by Fitzhenry & Whiteside, 195 Allstate Parkway, Markham, ON L3R 4T8.

Published in the United States by Fitzhenry & Whiteside, 311 Washington Street, Brighton, Massachusetts 02135.

www.fitzhenry.ca   godwit@fitzhenry.ca

10 9 8 7 6 5 4 3 2 1

Fitzhenry & Whiteside acknowledges with thanks the Canada Council for the Arts, and the Ontario Arts Council for their support of our publishing program. We acknowledge the financial support of the Government of Canada through the Canada Book Fund (CBF) for our publishing activities.

Library and Archives Canada Cataloguing in Publication
Compton, Anne, 1947-
Alongside / Anne Compton.
Poems.
ISBN 978-1-55455-227-6
I. Title.
PS8555.O5185A66 2013   C811'.6   C2013-900576-5

Publisher Cataloging-in-Publication Data (U.S.)
Compton, Anne 1947-
Alongside / Anne Compton.
[80] p. : cm.
Summary: Each poem is a conversation about the way in which the unlived life always walks beside us. It is a celebration of beauty which begins in the mind and wanders out into the garden and back again through the library, an unexpected love story that moves between the wild and the domestic.
ISBN-13: 9781554552276 (pbk.)
1. Canadian poetry — 21st century. 2. Love poetry, Canadian – 21st Century. I. Title
811.6080971 dc23 PR9199.4.C667A466 2013

Text Design: Karen Thomas/Intuitive Design International Ltd.
Cover Design: Daniel Choi
Cover Image: Detail from *Figures in a Divided Landscape* by Philippa Hunter
30 x 24 in. Mixed media on panel. Used with appreciation.

Printed and bound in Canada

for the dear ones – Aaron and Quentin, Theresa and Robbie

Contents

In the voice they have there

The library at all hours

Glossator

His Biography

...the conjunction of the mind, / And opposition of the stars.
Andrew Marvell

The Poet as Invalid

The surprise of summer lasted 'til August,
and an eightieth birthday.

We hedge a small life, he said. Elegantly sizing up
its boxwood form to left and right with his hands.

Even indoors stuff happens. Oddly colloquial.
Something of Prufrock in the Lear voice.

He's just back from reading a novel: Another
room to the house, as far as he's concerned.

For him, the towards force of tomorrow's been suspended.

He's got Still's Disease, moves stiffly, except
on the intact inner staircase, where his mind runs up and down.

There's sleep towards morning. The edges of it,
the short way back to everything he knows.

God's breath is the mist in the garden at daybreak,
a deer moving through it.

That's me talking. He believes in the deer.

He'd be the one to notice a man cupping a hand over a smoke;
a woman, freshening her lips in the café after lunch. No mirror.

I have two questions for my beloved: What weather would you wish for?
The day the rain takes the snow, that's the day I'd go.

And what words, at the last, would you look for? *There'd be a new idiom
to the rain, wouldn't there, an alluvial idiolect I'd hope to hear.*

Where creeks pool, yours will be the afterword.

Biography of the Poet

He's gone over the Bridge of Sighs, feet shambling the yellowed limestone.
Probably he's in one of the interrogation rooms. Only child, born to old parents,
he has a lot to answer for. Sins, *in petto*, to be named in one of the dead languages.

In his childhood, bread soldiers every breakfast, and cosseting. Her afternoons
in the sewing closet, making a winter coat for him, epaulettes in red.
What she wished for him – the armature of a king, or a legionnaire, at least.

He went out for words, went west. A newsagent on a passenger train:
Its rhythm, his rhythm. The wheel's incessant revolution – *lifelong, longlife* –
satisfied in a sequence of sonnets.

Found a voice in the newspaper's front page, impersonal as a dateline –
the only possible pattern now. The boy that was: Perishable as newsprint.
An inky lacuna in the biography: A dark pond at the centre of the hub city.

How many alleyways are there to an answer? You'd like to know –
wouldn't you – the last thing said, the morning of his last day: *I wish
someone would carry my sentences for me. They're getting so heavy.*

The human fear of night fowl comes into it, those nocturnals
who have heard it all – their finer ears – and nothing forgotten.

Past the pergola, he saw how the fog was holding up the heads of lilies,
reminding him of a weight he'd refused: A girl's head bent toward him.

The rowboat at the pier for after. Ladder down. I wanted his torment,
the entire history of him in my breath, breathing freely. The nearest-to, *this*.

It's not that I've gone out nights

It's not that I've gone out nights in men's clothing
or fallen in love with the women I followed. There's been so many.
I'm the last; least of them if looks count although, in his books, it's taste that
   matters.
He's someone I've kept going – a lie, if you like – invented and talked about
   with shopkeepers.
We chuckle at his fussiness, the just-so brands. The cigars I bring home from
   the tobacconist's, I smoke.
Also mine, the scotch and oysters we have on birthdays.
His falls on the twenty-second. *Here's to you, Ducky*. We toast the New Year
with spirits and market-fresh angelfish (his little joke). Smash the plates after.
      That dressing gown, men so admire, he wears all hours.
I've opened the door to them; closed it faster. Friggin' gossips.
He's become carbolic about poets: Paperhangers, according to him – all scraps
   and mucilage.
I swear there are pages concealed in the lining. Did I mention the suede glove,
a map of London inked on the palm? Not that he wears gloves any more,
   housebound as he is.
The reclusive are invulnerable to walls. He's writing an abstract on memory,
not his own, fair though it is, but the library without walls.
Some days, the ruins of the great royal one, Assurbanipal's, is the beginning.
Memory's the only immortality, he's fond of saying.
Your afterlife exists solely as thought – someone else's.
Opposite the undertaker at the funeral, the man in the dark overcoat is memory.
His work – housecalls – just beginning.

Seeing Things

From so simple a beginning endless forms…
most wonderful have been, and are being, evolved.
Charles Darwin

According to the physicists, the photoreceptors of the eye
have reached optimization: Practically perfect, they can't
evolve further. For what, you have to wonder, sight so keen?

With those good eyes, a woman's bound to notice beauty
when it enters a room, like I did that once and once is enough:

Photons of light blooming around you. Bones so elegant,
they testify to the first or final forms of things.

A voice summoning me to the surface, to attention –

to see, you said, how we are, like a child, surrounded
and adored by what we behold. Reciprocal fit.

I could say you were sent, opener-of-eyes. Unforeseeable,
your going 'though with no diminution of the light.

A harmed child, I was gutted and intensified: An attention

I can't let go, needing to name the beautiful in the least sprig.

Populus Alba: white poplar, in winter

What's light doing down there, in among the roots
of poplar, a crowd of them, and the way it travels
the bark up to incurved branches so that stems flare –
cupping its flitter in conical crowns. A convention of light
in a local thicket. Shoreside. Where murk leaves land,
where hereafter meets an hour, a copsewood lit to burning.
Twenty minutes, at most, imploring a wider wakefulness.

These pale ones – the faintest green trailing
through their sapwood – grasp what's here,
and on the verge of vanishing.

What the arborist calls inferior materials, we know as
utter regard, the trees' candlework at daybreak, our alba.

Hours into the meltday, you swore you could see snow shrinking.

Anatomy

All day I carry you inside me, your age and end –
the stooped fact of your dying. Near the vena cava,
a spine curved in sleep, not years. You are where
you should be, should have been
through the dividing decades: Those civil corridors
leading away from our alcove days – our avowals
that two right atria, so aligned, concur in rhythm.

I know the weight of a child, its stirring towards birth.
This is not that. This is the weight of the least words.

Thank-you note after a morning visit

He's up early for the morning's best brain.

The older you get, the softer the line between sleeping
and waking. Knife to plate, spoon to bowl. *Snick, snick.*

In making a visit, you need to tell a story, hear a story.
One of the proprieties, like a thank-you note after.

His talk's all about the self-similarity of forms
in nature. What Mandelbrot calls sensual geometry.

Naturally enough, I think of the geometry of bodies.
Ever the translator, and hopeful.

I've got on my gored skirt for the flare, a batwing sweater
of the wrap-around sort. Floaty. I'm after an angel's appearance.

June air's unimpeachable. Trees heave themselves about
in the fuzz of it. There are past-tense tulips in the garden,
but that's the way of things, and a scrubby green in the fields.

This is the setting, scene, costume of our visit, decades into separation.

We've lived opposite sides of the clock, crossed that one time,
late-century. Love is a short coat, worn once.

Cherishing, he claims, requires the cultivation
of indifference. You couldn't call it aloof.

Climbing down the stone steps, I've got gravity behind me.
I rhyme myself away: *You were my mutagen – my agent
of change. Didn't matter, you didn't stay.*

According to Eugenides, Love stories depend on disappointment.
That's the story I told. You'd heard it before but, then, I'm not an original.

It's plain as a wire hanger to me, but let's have
your answer: Do two hermetic lives make one lived life?

(In response to your talk, and by way of thanks,
I send you a list of overlaps – miserable comforters.)

Cities, now and then

Near the deanery, the pigeons are folded over the power lines like grey gloves
    to dry.
Next thing you know, the eye will make them out to pray. Every simile is short-
    sighted.

The natural fact, even without lift-off, transcends the gloss of words. Or as he
    put it –
taking to physics – *when you meet the fact, you touch infinity.* Graze of a
    kiss goodbye.

Frost-blankets rest on air: Floating islands, deceitful as the real ones. Everyone's
been exiled from one at least. That's the trouble with coasts. The shove-off's
    too easy.

Chimney smoke plumes high and white. Up and down the street – antiseptic
    houses.
In a frigid zone, even smell is deprived; the barrel vault of sky wants what
    you remember.

Northward, snow squalls huddle low to ground. Castor and Pollux near the
    quarter moon.

These are the patronal days of Lent, the sub-zero creak of trees and hours.
You're certain when you die, winter will have been the place you've lived most.

2

In another age and hemisphere, the ocean rose from its bed, set him ashore.
Shipwrecked on mine. The Phoenicians, whose city this first was, had no vowels.

Imagine the grinding sound of grief when water doesn't answer. Imagine fire,
sticks laid on gravel. But first picture the horizon – a ship, small as a bird in
    flight.

Think about the pigeons: How they roosted on the roofs of Carthage, then left.

Yellow Leather Gloves

Someone – was it you – reciting the banns: Impediment,
just cause, et cetera. The decades since
rehearsing the drawback.

Week of the moon down close, nearest it'd been
in years. The stars' pity eclipsed by the nearsighted
altitude of hope.

Ceremonial of the frost coming out, earth spongy.

You had on your Dublin coat for the weather.

April a-swank in spite of snow showers
soft as ticking   slantwise on the crocuses.
                         This is what happens
when you open early, the delusion of being filled.

Crossed a ditch and everything changed.

Past the chapel, the red horse of revelation
was a fox in a field, loping away. Further off,
a herd of sorrow nosing the snow for a grass blade.

That morning when you read out the Rilke – *And those
who are beautiful, / oh who can* retain *them* – I mistook
the word for *remain*, wanting the pledge of the ordinary.

I should have known from the wear pattern on your boots,
beauty is never conjugal.

Even so, what doesn't happen   remains:
The leathery close fit of it, hand in glove with the registry of fact.

The Biographer

A dark pond at the centre of the hub city.
The first ice that forms is always transparent –
a fleck-free window, revealing what's there,
way at the bottom. *You can lie at your length
on ice only an inch thick.* Its cold – a breastbone
away from the heart. This I did, looking into him.

Letters

You asked me to burn them, and I did. Took them down to the firepit by the river where grit is wet, charred logs shiny. November's all rain or was before this windiness. God, perhaps, airing the house before freeze-up. Words waft up from flame: *The cloakroom at four* and something about *the hands' transfer of heat*, which I'm reluctant to let drift over water. *The small bones of the wrist* also free now. Yours to me, an archaeology of carpal and ulna. Where mine are I don't know. I've learned since – that summer it was broken – the wrist is a joint complex.

What a word, wafted. So like to lofted, which we didn't. Or landed, either. Never shared house, yard, library. Books, yours and mine, spine by spine: Sleepers abed, until handed down from a shelf. *Nobody, not even the rain, has such small hands*, you would have read out to me one evening or another.

These letters a prologue. Or preamble, which allows for waywardness. In a box under a bed three decades. Slept across.

Like morning frost, the terseness of your vandalism note. The tilt of your writing, an awakening, arriving All Souls' Day.

Back then, I'd thought the alphabet would see us through.

On my own, I've reached the twenty-third, the *Oxford* headings, a guide. Here they are: washed up, water rat, weaken, etc. You're under the weather, according to your postscript. Who's not? Here on the coast, we're never over it.

November 2nd, he wrote

I want to go outside yesterday
and walk in the yellow All Souls' air.

Each day, the pale heads of trees lessen.

Bunched together and without definition,
leaves shift from écru to cream. Sfumato:

The effect of smoke if they were more that colour.

Not like the aggressive coming on of green,
or the stone certainty of limbs notching winter sky.

Used to be, in my village, there was scarlet.
Not here on the Esplanade des Invalides.

If you live alone, you want to be seen by someone
at least once a day. Spoken to. A loop of conversation –

however inane – can fish lovely and unlikely associations
out of torpor. I live in hope.

If you were here, you'd insist I see
the russeting of ivy on the church front.

The thing is, *Ivy ruins the wall it embraces.*
You take my meaning, don't you?

The biographer addresses the railing

This morning at eight, a doe in the garden stood quietly
while I spoke to her from behind the verandah railing.

Not trepified at all. *Shouldn't you be someone else?*
I asked, palming a windfall apple in her direction.

You have to wonder, of what evolutionary benefit the smile
if angels and animals can't return it. Its falsehood among
humans, infamous.   Let the apples speak for themselves.

How like to a snake the sentence goes, swivelling
through the underbrush, bent to the bitter fractals

of decaying leaves. Years have made a mush of what
came before. Still, the lowest layer's the richest.

I've been told the eyes of primates, us included,
evolved peripheral vision
in an environment of snakes. Also, declarative pointing.

The fruit-eaters' glucose-rich brain recognized *There, right there*

even as the snake moved off, a slither of elegant phrases.

If I did a forensic linguistics on your high-sided language,
would I find a way past the paling? That last time,

when you said, *Things seem to us of greater size from far
away than close up*, I'd guess you hadn't an object in mind.

Death, more likely. Or, maybe, a rebuke to my fondness?

He was a beautiful man.
What more needs to be said?
                    Molly Allgood

You were my South Shore and North Cape,
my East Point and West county lighthouse.
No man is an island, the poet said,
entire, complete; but I knew different.
Couldn't figure an approach. No cove,
creek or inlet. It's a fidelity of sorts,
the way I've compassed you. Decades,
and I'm down to the plainest words.
Your name is near, and everything.

The Garden, going on

Those who dispute about beauty don't know if it's in the mind or in things. Here, I'm saying things.

Eamon Stanley

Jacklight

A light used illegally as a lure when hunting or fishing at night

If you knew the end would you ever begin?

Of two people, one must be after – living
by praxis. Who's left behind lives another world,
not the past less one.
                              The perimeter daffodils –
a police tape circling the property. Trees
quizzical in April light.
                              Here in the house,
an old certainty among cups rattles the cupboard,
and those six fabric buttons for your good shirt –
futile fastenings in a copper bowl.
In the woods, last year turning to leaf mould.

By dusk, the forsythia's starting up: Its flash-bulb
flowering, penetrative. Someone abroad with a jacklight.
Below it, the tulips, in thirsty abundance, cupping
the warm rain. There is something in us, after us.

A Visitor to the Garden, April

i.m. JGC 1945-98

We are half-taught / our real names, from other lives.
Medbh McGuckian

In an unusually warm week with mid-day thunder (no rain)

and over all, a royal blue sky

two sorts of things bring wonder, and a third wrath.

The folded bud of the flower. You, coming into the garden

while I'm on my knees. Calling me by your new name.

Even as we praise the lilies' return –
those soon-to-be beauties, whose recurved flowers
have the backward bend of a bow –
there's a sniff of decay,
pallcloth laid down by a word, your word.

Shovel the bulb. Annul the sun.

Larger Blue Flag: Irises

Genesis 6:1-4

In the transplant season, wet spring, we lift the iris
set it down in a new bed. Its first leaves – a pair of them –
stiff and glossy, rise from the shoulder-shaped rhizome.
Not this year, but next, this dozen will bloom violet and veined.

Royal irises, they're called. In their maturity, tall and tufted
with what looks like hair. To us, scrabbling about in sweet loam,
they're simply flags, the larger and the lesser. Years back, naturally
enough, we settled on the showy-sized giants.
                                        Some say they're a warning –
something about young girls and the afterlife, how they can be led there.

While we work, sudden rain polishes the street pigeon-feather blue.
I'm one of those who sees wings everywhere. If I had a daughter,
I'd be on the top step calling her in, certain about what wings mean.

When the sons of God saw the daughters of men were fair,
they fathered children whose beauty – near to celestial –
took its form from loss. Scar tissue on the scapula. Minds
bent to rooms never seen and missed.
                                    Bearers of that bloodline
are liable to any messenger knowledgeable about stars

a map of the constellations on their many-fingered hands.

This daughter I don't have, I'd tell her. I'd warn.

When we're done here I'll alter the garden chart, colour in the new plot,
its diagrammatic blue belying the brutal cut that separates
one rhizome from another, the best of them snug in the transplant garden.
When it comes to beauty, everything's hurt in one way or another.
The ink-bruise at the pansy's centre probably has its own story.

Raspberries

for Aaron

genus, Rubus; family Rosaceae

To find them you must look *through*, not down.
Kneel or crouch in rose-rich leaves, pale green.

Upright shrub with perennial roots, suckering
underground. New growth, always at a distance.

A tincture made of its leaves, referred to as Woman's
Herb, is a relaxant during childbirth. The child unfolding.

Stems taller than you are shudder as you move.
The vines arterial from this position.

Fleshy fruit in filtered light: Its red, a benchmark for
one of the primary colours. Not watery, the way blood is.

In preserving, the colour will change. Anything spherical
is bound to be fragile.

2

According to the anthropic argument, certain features in
the universe appear uncannily "tuned" in favour of life.

Seen from below, raspberries on the vine could be its musical
score or a contractor's diagram for wiring a house.

3

For my fortieth birthday, you gave me a globe.
May the world be at your feet, you said, and it was

while you were growing.   I gave you into the world
when I should have kept you close. Like an oblate child

to a monastery for his singing voice. Years later I'm in the kitchen,

pouring sealing wax on what's less than what was.

Rain, Summer

After two dozen days, no one was counting;
the names of the months remained unspoken.

Steadiness was a property outside.
Children within doors said it was the same rain.

Their elbows, on sills, left watermarks in wood.

Possibly they were right.
After a while, anything falling couldn't be seen.

Hadn't we always been here? Time, a stalled ocean we crossed with ox-barge
    slowness.

The tallest in the garden – monkshood and campanula – took to the ground,
unable to hold up their heads, their unopened blooms. We understood this.

Raindrops, forgetting their liquidity, piled on leaves like winter snow.
The saturation point was passed without ceremony.

All that standing around, for what?

Once, in an hour's sunshine, grackles stepped through the lawn's long grass.
Some few remarked their keel-shaped tails, iridescent crowns. Undulating.

Voices, as from a distance, altered in the damp. Words under umbrellas –
rising to us – had a new timbre. Something unearthly.

It got so we saw it indoors, a thickening of air in closets.

If you were up early enough, you could catch
the daybreak storms, a last reminder of natural light.

To Him who made the great lights, we asked for it.

Heat Week

On the final night of six combustible days,
many suffered falling dreams: Walked rafters,
stumbled back from a well-head, a wharf-end.

Those lucky enough to awaken gravitated to
windows – unclad, discurtained – for the least
breeze. It was nothing to see bodies in lamplight

high above lawns, lit by a moon italicizing
the worn luxury of the peony. One night short of full.

Disturbed by the memory of watermelon, a clergyman
followed thirst out of sleep. Floundered on the steps
of a barrel-vaulted staircase where heat – shaped to
its curvature – leant like fate on the nape of his neck.

The thinnest, all through the week, felt heavy
inside their clothes: The word *liturgical* occurring
to them in reference to the most customary gesture.

The world, several degrees askew, inferred a different body.

Homo Erectus came down from the trees, slept on
the ground, getting a first good night's sleep –
those slow-wave dreams altered his cognition.

Caves, huts, houses ensued. Basilicas and mosques.

You have to wonder why houses aren't oftener
guarantors against the force that gets indoors the mind.

Signs

Early morning, fall stops at the August inn,
makes a long-stay reservation. Nods approvingly
at the spiderweb trellising the verandah. Says
I'll be back for good, three weeks Friday.

Meanwhile he's off to count crows in pairs,
set a limit to the Michaelmas daisies purpling
a roadside ditch. The V-engine of geese, his vector.

He could be Hermes, the god of going-between,
wayfinding between the still-living and the dead,
us and everything to come.

Morning's down in the garden with secateurs,
beheading the roses. Probably, his daughter. You can
tell by the profile. Hawkish nose and serpentine hair.

Fog withdraws its curtain as if all this were a balcony
or bedstead. August lies down there after lunch,
cool cloth to her forehead.

There've been lawnmower afternoons all through
the summer, their somnolent purr over the grass,
a comfort.

These days, though, grassblades don't add a cell.
She's feeling their parch. At its apex, she says, a woman's
life is a diminishing thing: Crest and slump, the same.

And then a traveller arrives, lick of frost in his gorgeous mouth.

Nights back, the Perseid shower should've been warning enough:
Its blips and pings a bit like music, a dying fall.

Sojourn: biblical in the garden

[OFr < L. *sub*-, under + *diurnus*, of a day < *dies*, day]

We're putting down the garden. Wrapping
the rose – burlap and twine. Liming the hellebore.
An ark-before-the-flood attitude: Ararat, our spring.

The early and the late rains, a curtain
not in our control, a framing device for the drama
that'll lift us off our feet, set us down in a new world.

The cows, meanwhile – mindful of the earth's magnetic
field – all graze in the same direction, a north-south
alignment. Still on pasture this strange November

and near to the trees where the field is greenest –
economists of the vice versa: *All flesh is grass*.

Those withering lines we call to mind, an ability we have
since we haven't theirs: *When* and *where* in their pelts.

Likely, the boxwood hedge we're trimming will last
our lifetime and three more besides. Do the math
on the bristlecone pine if you care to. Shift the ladder.

Every day tells its own direction.
We're just feeling the wall for a light switch.

Sojourners travelling room to room, we're off the steps
in the duplicitous garden, thinking we have an effect.
House shoes in the muck.

Imagining, the gardener

In fall, we're working for the next spring.
Winter, a salt mine where we store our best images:
Delphinium and larkspur, those competing blues
and the in-between of allium. Bulb, another word for hope.

A gardener breaks a pod (poppy) over a fresh bed,
imagines its tissuey red hailing the campanula:
Semaphores, because we haven't language enough, or skill,
for the way Death draws us down to the cot in the stormcellar

'til we can hardly resist his *hush, hush*. We're that near again
to his awful authority. But for their rising in us, we might

stay there. Time was, we assailed heaven's blue
with a radio transmitter. When Babel failed, it was left
to the winged commuters to bear the death-defying news.
That kind of talk takes a lot of oxygen. Now we're bereft,

and even the moon is moving away from us.

Escape from his seduction, less and less likely.

We had two vectors – hope and compliance – and one
of them's disappeared. Only the seeds are unappalled.

Haar: frost smoke off the North Atlantic

Even the words *overcast December day* have slack in them,
a falling away sound. Someone's taken an eraser to colour:
Everything's pavement grey. Absolute, I'd say, is the word
for bare trees, and the river, icing up, looks a cast-off shield.
Crows, in their military coats, are undeterred. They're warriors –
scouts perhaps – for the withdrawn king whose wounds turned
his mind: Smirch of ash, his sense of it. Grey's the one colour
that's its own complement. Nothing answers.

Even so, there's a three-foot scud of frost rabbiting over the ground,
and yesterday – I suddenly remember – on the Lower Cove Loop,
didn't a fox cross in front of me, lagging his bushy tail? A dancer
who didn't get away by dawn. Carouser, glad of the frost cover –
the *haar* in from the harbour. Houses, up to their knees in it,
are off their foundations, or so it seems. Down there – at ground
level – the world's tipsy with quickening light.

Those who hibernate, those who don't

The vulpine light of a full moon in February –
taking its drama from the dark – disturbs more
than what's filtered by day. Sleepers underground,
who know the risk, put an iron-rich element between
themselves and that look:
                              The way it thumbs through
memories – drops some, digests others – mashes together
your thinking, your neighbour's, in whose talk,
tomorrow, you'll hear your own speech pattern.

                    2

The red fox hunts in a northerly direction,
the earth's magnetic field a reference, a visual pattern
in its right eye. The grid's least blur: Sign of a shrew
or mole tunnelling in snowdrift. Without those optics,
the down-below's invisible to us.
                              We might as well
be the mouldywarp: The full moon slyly marking
a thermal pattern on snow-crusted roof. The self,
sunk in sleep, as liable to dissolution as body heat.

The tree in winter

The tree in winter is near to pure form –
sonnet without content, ghazal in grey.
Sap sunk to root, fibrous root thirsting its way
to water table, while bare limbs conform
to loss; no conduction can be inferred.
Still, there's an underground to everything:
The way your absence, even now, is moving
in some element unamenable to word
or syntax. If lingual, let it be what stones
hear: I don't want to know *if* you recant,
or *why*, the beauty you lifted vein by vein
through me. Knowing only, I'll not be that again.

Footwork in Four Seasons

Mark this down. March 8th: Out early, saving daylight.
Spring's washing her eyelids: Suds drip from eaves.
Hillock – where the blue spruce stands – exposed:
Stub of daffodil pushing through. Otherwise,
snow in mauve and grey over the yellow grass.
On the St. Croix, alewives leap over the fishway to spawn.

2

All summer the smaller plants move *con il sole*,
bending to the present tense, unaware light'll
withdraw, wreck them to the root. The thick
of the pretty. The quaking aspen knows different.

3

Shocked, she runs the word up the stairs,
her hair unwrapping from its pins, draws
a breath on the landing. The window there –
mullioned and crack-paned – corroborates
fire; Men burning the stalk of the year.

4

How like to us the trees look. Clenched.
A boy in a footbrace, the arch of the root
in hard frost, ankle deep in snow. Mute,
the forebearing mind can't put a foot forward:
White's a corner you can't see around.

In the voice they have there

...the sound of things becoming / what they never will again.
John Glenday, "At Innernytie"

Fire and Grammar

How is it you can miss what you still have?
Earlier versions crowding the chesterfield –

agrammatical. Backward run the sentences.
Broca's area of the brain unable to manage.

Lordy, lordy, where's the rapture gone?
What comes through the night – sensible in rainwear
and step-ins – a has-been. No heat to it whatsoever.

The past's a train – tracks torn up. Rabbits and rodents
overrunning the rail-bed.

Everyone's late to nostalgia: It's where you have to go
on foot. Whinging over the cinders.

It's not possible to be active in the past,
and passive sentences are a tedious think-through.

Headlamp to my hurrying feet, the future: What a mistake that was.

So busy with the finish, I forgot to burnish
the everyday brass: Sconce either side the daylit mirror.

Mirrors are lateral thinkers: Reverse left to right. Likewise,
the left brain talks to the right foot. Verticality, so far.

When you're done for good, the one that's full-length
shows the image upended.

Wittgenstein's duck-rabbit has to be this or that,
but what happens when the barnyard empties?

Another way of putting it: Soon as it comes
into being, the past's a fiction. The one you loved,

relocated there: Flensed to a few words, a paragraph maybe.
And yourself? Already, someone's fingering the spine.

Pictures

The future has a frame on it.
Its long-looked-for contents stand a ways off.
We'll agree to anything so long as it's behind glass.

The authoritative present hands us forward,
down a gallery, underlit except for pot lights.
At its narrow end, Time-the-Curator – cravat

and gloves – removes the frame, deglazes
the scene and we're in the room of it, unable
to sort what's shattered: Figures so like our selves.

Think that up if you can, hisses his assistant,
a woman carrying what could be an exhibition
catalogue or agenda book. A purse-sized mirror.

Steeple

Even in this room, the unlived life's a draught of ionized air –
counter to the ventilated dust particles, the cross-current
of holy images –
                    a conductive path parallel to
streetside powerlines. Possibilities that failed,
or didn't quite. And though the preacher says, the celestial's

a new body called to the banquet – the corruptible
sweetened and sanctified – it could be heaven's a live current
left over from our refusals, a retrograde mourning attracted to
the highest point of a lifetime, as the preacher would have it.

Which is why there's a finial on the spire, the work
of a steeplejack who knows the ways of a lightning strike,
how it must be diverted, brought to ground. Its principle:
Attract and intercept   so the crackling regrets

crowding the pew won't be vitalized by heaven's voltage.

Flight

What's more perverse than the paradoxical dressing
of the dead? Hired men straightening your father's cuff.
Rouging up the omega absence – wide as a country pond –
settling on your mother's face.

If, by its mass, a body can warp time and space,
what can't the sensational spirit do, vacating ours,
bearing with it so much touching upon our senses?

It's an evolutionary truth, everything's made to fit
with something else: The long-tongued moth matched
to the deep-throated flower.
                              The nectary of their loves,
where we sipped sweet water, is need-by-design.

2

They take with them the last aromas of a room
voices held in the semicircular canal of the ear.
The precise weight of someone's hand on a limb,
translated with alar speed to some new language.

The waters above the heavens have been drained,
a boggy backwater, but the iconography of flight
still suits the landscape-emptiness left to us.

We try to keep them near, pretend they're present
while we eat the burial cakes. When what's gone
is parcels of ourselves. First thing mornings, the mind's
a vacant pond. Its surface tension scumming over.

Rope Handles

The day of the linens in spring is a set-aside:
Every bed stripped, and the blanket press emptied.
A New Year's of sorts. There'll be savarin for supper,
brook trout and greens on a red-rimmed platter. An oval.
The table's one too. Every day, something shows itself.
I mark it down: Line times colour.

Baskets, five or six large ones, stacked in the hall.
Wet laundry loosely folded. The back door open,
its sunshine an umber over all that white.
The person who's to carry it to the clothesline
isn't here yet. The wash done, the others are having tea.
That'd be another room.
                              Can't see it from here —
bottom step of the backstairs. I've stepped down to see
April's blue surprise, a shade of sky known as copen.

You said I wasn't to go back there, but this is before,
when the ceremonial of the least chore timed our days.

The light over the wicker work's gone copper.

The past does that, Colours with a changeful light.

There's no stopoff, you know, no sieve analysis in how
we're made. The carbon of our ancestors is in us.
Their dispersal, our daily breath.

What the construction worker said

last: n. [from the AS], a form shaped like a foot,
used by shoemakers in building or repairing shoes.

– Mountains lose a centimetre and a seventh
every year. Hills round off to the nearest nought.
In its stone foundation – granite and gravel –
the house too seeks sea level, slides some annually.
You see it in shelves – how books come to the edge,
sag in the spine, ready to empty themselves in air.
There'll come a day, load-bearing words will crumble,
revert to sand on the seafloor of sleep. *Footing*,
he said, is a misnomer. Angels alone lift their own weight.

When he jacked up the house, a child's shoe slid from
the space between walls. The last, used in its making,
tucked under the tongue. Harbinger of a future
a hundred years gone.

John and me, skating

for JGC

The pond-ice, the river-ice, hardly held our long-legged stride.
Hatless and hero-heated, we stormed winter storms: The wind
at our backs rounding the river bend, into the open, where bonfires
burned. The houses up the harbour were Samothrace or Samarkand:
Cities we'd know, for sure, someday. For sure, everything everywhere
waited for us. We were twelve, we were fourteen. Love hadn't found us,
our bodies had: Wonders of muscle and bone. We were flight, we were
fluency – such lank-limbed lovelies – truant in the in-between time.
What couldn't we do with looks lately learned, our spoon-bending
minds? We owned it all: Stars almighty, the unfenced distance,
and the river route to the four-points horizon no one else knew of.
When we were perfect we weren't aware, and took it for granted.

It was windows all around in the sibling-centred universe.

Bread

They are hungry when they arrive, a hunger wide and deep, no edge to it. Where they are, there isn't an edge to anything. Travellers, more tired than hungry, but even that is an ache not a need. Each one's given a drink of milk, scalded and cooled, stirred with honey. They're the ones who've arrived late-afternoon, in the quarter light. They've no memory of the way through, and the weariness slipping from them has a history years off.

Hardest for her is the letting go. Sitting there, on the slat-wood bench, her fingers worry its grain. She's recalling the shape of a child's skull, how she pulled him into her lap whenever he came near, his body fitting hers exactly – cup and contents, she'd thought – her chin on his head.

Let everything go. Everyone.

She remembers now: The taxi, late-model brown van. Why, anyway, had she been in that taxi? Oh, yes, the ride from the garage. The Corolla in for a re-fit. The van lifting on impact, the driver's arm pressing her to the seat as if to hold her safe. And the tilt of the fall.

There's a stoop to the tall one pouring milk. What she hands the restive woman could be the cup of kindness. Or water from the well of forgetting.

In the voice they have there, the man nearest asks after the place. Heaven, perhaps? He imagines room after room leading to a main one, but he'd be wrong. *The antechamber is all.* Words, few and simple, misunderstood. He doesn't have to. The stooped figure touches eyelids, lips. Sleep, a child's sleep, covers him.

Evening and morning, the first day.

Rose

The mid-day woman you meet in the grain field will ask for a story. That story could save your life. She found me at the fence-end, all barb-wire and briars, so I told her about Rose.

Birds came down to her. Not something I believe happens, really, except in books. A boy, maybe, in the Weimar forest long ago. Nonetheless, we're on a path in Scattery Park, our shoulders bumping from the narrowness of it, telling stories of the summer and glad to be in our jackets because of the coolness in the air. Smell of fallen apples. Ahead of us on the path a crow landed, coming in like an airplane, straight for the runway. She went down on one knee, her hand out. The crow waddled toward her. With her index and middle finger she touched the crown of its head. When she stood up it cawed and flew off at a right angle to her. Even from where I was, off the path on the other side, I could feel its wing beats. We went on as far as the ancient apple tree, where the useless apples had fallen, and turned back. Another time we were down at the river and she was stretched out on her back on one of the flat-topped boulders there, knees pulled up and arms under her head, concentrating on the sky. I was at the river's edge, skipping stones. At my feet I had a pile of flat ones, the right weight and oval-shaped. I twisted round to her with my at-least-eight-that-time voice, and a crow was standing on the plaid lining of her coat where it'd fallen open around her. Its wings were slightly raised as if it couldn't decide whether or not to rise. She didn't move or anything. When it flew up, it crossed over her body. Other times, in the woods, Rose'd be walking along, a crow moving branch to branch ahead of her. She'd slip a hand into her skirt pocket and palm something and quick as anything, it'd swoop down to it. No break in her stride or talk. Since she's been gone, I go to the river alone, feel no connection to any of it, not the bleached logs, the Michaelmas daisies in among the pebbles or the yellow yarrow buttons at the edge of the woods behind me. It must be how it feels on the deck of an ocean-going liner with the sea going by. The endless melancholy of it.

That's not a story, the old woman said. It's an impression. There isn't anybody boiled or flensed or flailed in it. I am, I said. Scanted of what I had, and went back to the house.

Cab Ride, Paris

Boys on the sidewalk, young men really, walking their bikes
one hand on the crossbar. Casual. As if the bikes were wolfhounds.

Yesterday's early snow, an extra curb between sidewalk
and street, framing the solemnity of the single file. Thunder
snow, it's called: Weather's sudden shift lit up like revelation.

Because the cab pulls away, I don't see them lean
their bikes against a shop, and one after another, walk in.
Or, at the end of the block, mount the bikes, ride off.

In another time, the four of them – before
a reviewing stand – sat erect in their saddles,
their head-gear stowed, hair to their shoulders.
Or, they walked at the horses' heads – a hand on
the bridle strap – leaving the arena, the games done.

In this or that century, I've seen them up close.
Dark, non-committal eyes – their interest off
somewhere else – acknowledging my glance
with a nod. Courtesy, as practised as a sword arm.

Their kind have fused will and body, an infant discipline
they're born to. But I have – in my time – held them,
lulled them, breathed the talcum of their sleeping,
knowing even then they'd be slipping from me. Sons,
I say, to the darkening cab, be as you are – ages becoming –
the world a backdrop to your inscrutable bearing.

Allegory: The body addresses the heart

Seems it's just ourselves – the pair of us –
here at the river's turning, door of the boatshed ajar.

The cargo afloat on the tide's nothing you'd recognize.

Nor does the canticle of gravel underfoot
sound anything like the generosity of rain
we heard down valley. Or upslope, where
we left the children, those who had the most of you,
making their headstrong way through the custodial foliage.

That strength of hills behind us now.

On our layover in the mountains, did you notice the quiet –
how everyone's gone from the mind's winter palace?
Not a thought for the fallen roof, the uprooted furniture.
The crowd of them off somewhere.   Not even an old one in the library.
Remember how consolatory they could be in foul weather,
and how, just a little, you'd envy their cryptic remarks.

Which is likely why I was slow to their smirk:
Even the sweetest rain cannot refresh cut grass.

Let's face it, We've been hospitable to strangers,
allowed them the best room, unaware they'd vacate
when they saw us nearby in oldest clothes
and worst wear: Habit had of a lifetime.

Still, if they were about, what wintry irony they'd make
of the door ajar, the small manoeuvres left us now.

The library at all hours

Whoever has no house, here are walls accounted double.

Whoever has lost his way, follow the ladder to the vaulted roof.

Whoever has no table, let him have one here, his own lamp to light.

Whoever has no coat, curtains are close-drawn at all hours.

Inscription over the entrance of the Santa Maria Library, Rome

Reading Around

The library's a building without mirrors, or all mirror.
Bookworm: Some larval version of who you could be.

If silence is the loudest speech, the reading room's full
of tongues: Lick of spit, the speed of the page-turners.

The bent blond head of the reader, an elation of light
on his neck. *He's the servant of beauty, not beauty itself.*

Hard to resist the centimetres where the hair curls.

Reading, it seems, lessens the sorrow of being awake.

The books on the shelf are open with themselves. The heart's
a short-term loan. Circulation, a principle and front desk.

Fell down a phrase, she said, explaining how
the book she'd returned saw her to sleep.

Sleeping, waking, reading – the night verbals.
The coordinating conjunction rarely works for me.

There's a relief globe on an oak stand: Not a world I'm familiar with.

Look here, he said, *how can there be so many books and no
eternity in which to read them?* It's libraries that show us
what heaven could be.
                              Imagine the chairs there. The due-date stamp.

Thought into word. Skittish until captured.

What's between the wild and the domestic? The garden's
one way of thinking about it; the library, another.

Minds in books, books in library, the library opposite
the cemetery: Isn't that the truth, though?

Plovers

I followed him through the world, which wasn't far. Up dune and down. The shore was library and lab to him. Me tagging along.   The cosmic speed limit, he'd say, wasn't always constant. Can't have been. Think of the rate of expansion right after the Big Bang. And I would.

Think, that is, of his gesticulating hands, his ship-prow face. Was there ever a man of such forwardness? You're right about that, Ducky, I'd murmur. Or, Tell me more, in my real-girl voice.

His words were pears quartered with a sharp knife, razor-edged and juicy. The wind would be pushing one way and then another, a confetti of gulls over us, and the talk wouldn't stop. Singularity, cosmic soup, whatnot.   I was always hungry. One time, to humour me, he brought take-out. We ate it on the railroad tracks on the way to the shore. Crows stalking the wrappers. A dish of artichokes or sorrel, his idea of a meal.   A great galumphing girl, I had no idea why I was wanted there: Dust trail to his meteor.

There were times we smelled of bayberries. The hollows of the dunes were full of those bushes and sometimes we'd lie out of the wind and he'd do voices. Byron, he'd say? Or Coleridge? And a poem would follow. A different voice, plaintive as the plovers', up from the Carolinas to nest, sand-flea pale so as not to be seen. The world was in him. I went indoors.

Her river, mine

A memory you come on by mistake: Is it best not to mention it?

An affliction from reading, perhaps? Already, I'm older than she was
in the fifth diary, its pages prophetic of another hand in the final lines.

The speckled shore stones dark from the current
that pushes in, pulls out.   She cut across.
The wet skirt, wrapping her legs, was a resistance.

Before that, the choice of stones.

I've read her books to find which ones. Every word weighed
for its anchorage. The pocket handkerchief crushed under.
Jacket over the cardigan because it was a cool March morning.

In *The Waves*, I'll leave a cupboard of old clothes when I die.

As you say, she absorbs me. Mind on loan,
but what if you can't borrow back?

Stones are rocks put to use. Or is it the other way around?

                              Uselessness lying about,
another way of thinking over this pebble-strewn waste.

I return the books to the library and am not lighter. In her country,
though not in mine, bodily weight measured in stone: Imperial Mass.

I've dressed too long in these diaries: Over my head and down
to my knees. The hobbling close fit of them.

Appeal to the librarian. She's expert at calling books to mind.

Beatrice

She wants floors without coverings;
awnings where the doors should be.
There are days she can abide a trestle table,
chairs off their wall hooks,
so long as she can see past them to the floor.

                              The library ladder unfolded.

She's up early for the daybreak of planked wood,
the scrub of uncluttered space: Minimum's
a mirror to amplify light, showing off the gills
and scales she sees in floorboards. Or imagines.

Mirror carp, dozens of them where she comes from,
making a cheval glass in sun-struck water. Swim
even in their sleep. Christ's fish, with the world on its back.
I come from where I crave to be: Words to lift a roof off.

Seckel pears on a credenza, her only concession.

Encyclopaedia of Child Care, 1904

Fires banked, the house cools at night.
The air of forests and a frozen river enters.
In its chill, sleepers dream fur-lined tents, caves,
not unlike where they are, under down and wool.

Bare foot to floorboard, a child flits down a hall:
She's out for the air, the jab of cold through feet,
its lash along the spine. *Spruce*, she thinks. *Muskrat*.
Eager to breathe air not breathed before. *These others*.

At sunrise, someone will stir embers,
kindle anew the heat that remains in stoves –
one in each main room, through three storeys.
The box heater in the bathing room lit first.

Another will bathe the child, pick off twigs,
chafe hands. Boil wood ash in water – lye
for her chilblained feet. Later, apply almond salve
to chapped lips; a poultice, in case of convulsions.

The child's mother blames a mishandling at birth:
Clothes put on over the head, instead of safely drawn
up over the feet. Or, had they – she can't remember –
failed to carry her, the first time out, up a stairs or street.

Whichever, she's turned the wrong way 'round – back
from where she's come. Or – and this is the worst –
she's a come-again. Not theirs, really. A night-born
on the darkest day of the year. The February sun stokes

a faint light. The child's father, who's fond of saying,
Let every man sweep the snow from his own door
untroubled by the frost coating his neighbour's tiles,
hasn't the least notion of the frost that goes over his own floors.

Natural History Museum

It's a braw bright night. / The wind's in the West, / And the moon shines bright.

Beatrix Potter

Her childhood limited to a London attic and chaperoned walks:
Up there – uncaged – a menagerie of friends of the animal sort.
Watched what was near with watercolour eyes: A ciphered journal
thick as a papal archive.

As to fungus spores, she had a theory and drawings by the thousand.
Tut-tut snapped the professionals: Shirtfronts agile as a swivel snare.

In her stories, shoes and galoshes go missing, but always
the animal escapes: Rabbit, home to bed, *lippity-lippity.*

Frog off to supper with Sir Issac Newton and Alderman
Ptolemy Tortoise.
                     You have come the best of the year,
we will have herb pudding and sit in the sun.

Wrote her way into hills and *a wandering habit*. Rumour was,
she burned the fox pelt muff left her by her mother. Silver.
Its silkiness due to guard hairs that protect in any weather.

Picture Books

It's summer and the cat sits on the sill;
the child, on the verandah bench, opens
a book of pictures. The citron smell
of mowed lawn – *alla prima* on a still life.

Somewhere inside, my second son
sleeps a traveller's repose – a father's calm,
now he's home. Generations set down
like chess pieces – queen, knight, pawn.

As usual, I'm half away from here, scanning
hazy hayloft air for a boy walking a beam.
Where it began, or ended, that *nostos* I'd happily forgo
for the good of a boy reading ahead

if only that other, somersaulting through chaff –
high-crying my name – hadn't astigmatized sight.

From London, by way of Montreal, March

Thaw without rain, frost without snow,
we're suspended between squall and renewal.
The river ice thinned to an eyelid, a cobalt blue
beneath. Cloudy as cataracts some mornings.
Yesterday, home from London, we eased off
the windows' weatherstripping, inviting
into the house the evening light
we'd seen staggering down the St. John: Luciferous
after the nun-grey sky – slate, would you call it –
of Lachine. Their trees – the willow especially –
dusty birds' nests, as we ascended.

In airports, on planes, we sneak-survey
the books passengers open. Who anyway reads
Adorno in transit? *Insomnia*, the traveller tells me,
is the fault of modern buildings. How tiresome is that?
Weren't they sleepy in the middle ages? I ask. Biscuit
crumbs falling into *Heresy*, bent out of shape with
marginalia. If there are mice breeding in cargo,
they'll find the cabin – steward and passengers gone –
a down-to-earth bliss. *The Bishop's Man*, diagonal to me,
past oblivious to the coffee cart. A paisley scarf wrapping
a clerical collar. In 2-D, *Good to a Fault* falls asleep
over a page, and, my God, the man in aisle forward
is thumbing the *Oxford Dictionary of Current English*.
I should tell him, opportunistic pathogen live at the edges.
This game, the gaiety of being between places, or
the anticipation of home
                              where there's a mauve tint
to morning light, and even the snow mould, patching
the garden – *typhula incarnata* – repeats the flush of it.

And though last year's leaves, rigged firm by frost,
are an immobile memorial, wild thyme's pushing through,
reminding us of the gravestones tumbled by tree roots
in Highgate. How pushy past death the energy that's in us.
There's a reason *is risen* is the verb tense of Easter.

Estate Library

The day makes its way to evening. It always does. Its one and only consolation.

Ah, here we are again. The hallway where the light fixture failed long ago.
Small triangular mirror, off a ship, spelling out *What is the speed of the dark?*

While we sleep, the river is silting its banks. Wood lengths, stacked floor to
  ceiling
in the outside porch, settle some. Meanwhile, those upright sleepers, the trees,
  recall

the understories they've taken up, preserved for some future form – booklength.

I thought of Thomas Hardy's library: How he'd written *Max Gate* on every
  volume
he'd collected. We put our name to words, as if we owned them. Estate that
  survives us.

About libraries, I've discovered, the opposite's also true: *Show me a library
  and I'll show you
what concealed but couldn't hold him*. Words, words: We're in them, or we're
  not.

What I wouldn't let in the door, came in under a different heading: Stranger still,
he was waiting – blurry in a crumpled raincoat – at the foot of the escalator.

Let's call it a gangplank for the similitude. So, I stepped off the ship, and onto
his coast – fog and evening flurries. Everything looks its best when wet. Words
  in close.

Using the vocative, I've asked and asked for a different mind, one that doesn't
work in reverse: Flock of starlings moving counterclockwise. Little bastards.

Centuries ago, painters discovered spatial recession. How did they miss time's?

The day's a woman, working her way through afternoon chores to reach her
  grief.

End-papers

The invalid in summer rests on the verandah in the cool hours:
Morning and evening, a rug around his knees, book in hand.
The bordering shrubbery – wigelia, forsythia, honeysuckle – spurt and
sputter roof-high, tangling into the leant-low branches of red maple,
constructing pedways crossed by birds and squirrels: The hundreds' world
he favours. The book unread. He writes the names of the householders –
chickadee, nuthatch, cardinal – on the blank back pages, sketches flight
silhouettes.
      At this stage, he says to himself, the mind shoves off
from the body easily. There must be a calculus to this: The body
lessening, the mind unmooring. No regret in the going-off.

A mourning dove walks the verandah railing. Ruby-throats
in the honeysuckle.
      His marginalia doesn't allow for
the ugly words – shrub, creeper, privet – we have for this world,
the one lit and in motion that he watches from the shade porch.
His line of sight, leaf-limited: How it should be, he figures,
shortstay guest at the world's matrimonial – the brooding, hatching,
hovering-over busyness.

In the pollen afternoons, he's in a blind-drawn upstairs room,
mind itemizing sounds. Underneath the hum of traffic, he hears
whistling wing sounds, a swift's *chippering*. He's never been
so stopped, so near-to. A world revolving his standstill.

Glossator

I did step into another's garden for these flowers
although they are of my own gathering and making up.
Isabella Whitney, *Sweet Nosegay*, 1573

Shoreland

Horses down in the meadow, just a few degrees above snow....
If the door were open, I'd listen to creek water
And think I heard voices from long ago,

                        distinct, and calling me home.

The past becomes such a mirror – we're in it, and then we're not.

                              Charles Wright

When word of an ancestral misdemeanour arrives
bloodlines shift
                 an unseen ropy helix unwinds:

When the past pulled away,
                   I was close in to shore
counting lighted windows in the tall house, one each
for the brothers gathering Irish moss for garden cover,
the sisters moving through the house with lamps, wicks
tilted northward: Settling down the day and the season.
The cattle, milked and fed, going down on their knees
as they always did. The stalled ox. Cadential chaff.
Horses down in the meadow, just a few degrees above snow.

In the past safely ashore, everything would be where
it's supposed to be
                 visible as a field crop at harvest,
its undulation of colour, umber to ochre, when you
see it from afar. Having wearied prosaic days among
strangers, I wanted to see them – the faithful ones –
run to and fro like sparks among stubble. Shine.
Sure as Solomon, safe as houses:
                   Isn't that how it goes?
Memory's antecedent, *mindful*: How amply it terraces and
tenants. Not that it's possible to go inshore, reach the house,
where, if the door were open, I'd listen to creek water.

An inland quickfrozen in affection, unchangeable.
Nothing there
        the watcher doesn't know, or can know further.
Her position, offshore.
          Seasons descend in memory, but these
are neither serial nor calendric. The creek icing up that once
stands for every late autumn. The rambler vine, espaliered to
the garden wall, bronzed with frost. Holiest of the aromatics,
the rosemary, stays 'til solstice. The past's a sacred geography,
indoors each of us, a mordant fixing its colours. The gestures
of those we loved are like that too, singular. Making me think,
I heard voices from long ago
             distinct, and calling me home.

January thaw – its light, towards evening, smoulders a dim
yellow, a sulfuric shade.
          Heat enough to waken wintering
wasps, an awakening that's unwanted, like words out of time
blurring familiar voices.

You can't enter the past – it's true – but there are towlines
that steady you alongside. Their unravelling
           renders tomorrow indistinct.

The future's cleated, slopes upward, a gangway
             up and away from.
The mind far out in a fogbank: Can't see a face in front of you.
Shoals and seabirds, no land to speak of.

The past becomes such a mirror – we're in it, and then we're not.

Waste Places

the white rooms and the apple-scented doors
enclose spirits distilled from sorrows
that only curtains could understand
only cabinets could possibly know
                                    Don Domanski

Except for a spiral staircase hanging off a half-floor
the house is down to its thwarts and struts –
wall cladding, closet, cupboard stripped or fallen.
If you risked those stairs you'd see, storeys below,
vegetation scalloping over collaborative cellar dirt,
vines climbing up out of ferns, fireweed and vetch.
The whole, a solarium of no one's construction:
Herbage, in cahoots with the sun, taking it over.
Steps, loose in the air, belie the white rooms of memory,
the apple-scented doors, ornamented long ago by a lover.

Where squirrels have cached chestnuts, trees erupt
from an overgrown garden. Creeping plantain rises
from moss, the moss fingering tree roots. Wildings,
escaped from an orchard, twist themselves around
the remains of a fieldstone fence.
                              The mind, in its
isolation, eludes such entanglement: The symbiotic
verdure that comes of sinking into loss   the earthy
mulch of sorrow. If you don't go through the narrow,
how can you come into the broad   the overly full that
decay proposes when spirit's distilled from sorrow?

Hardest for us, the digging in that roots do
in waste places. The mind finds refuge in the feasible:
What to make of the timber? Sizes up a carrying beam,
calculates the horizontal of a lintel where, oddly enough,
an apple wood detail remains intact and you are within

the scent of it: The past searching the present. And this
is the other way, not down but back: A verbal furnishing
of the house. Walls, closets, cupboards. The windows
glazed again and lifted. Open to the fields' breathing
in ways that only curtains could understand or a lover know.

Imagination, let's say, is a set of stairs. There's a landing –
if you reach it – that'll situate you at a different level, not here
or there, but in a passage between. Remember how the halls
ran close and complicated: Narrow corridors crowded
with rumour, each one a paragraph.
                                    The reap and sow
of husbandry happened here, and what they raised up,
remains. Words too, once spoken, drift among wildings.
A woman, setting milk to cool on a cellar floor,
told herself secrets, whisperings overheard by a cupboard,
secrets only cabinets could possibly know.

Notes

"Biography of the Poet" alludes to Marshall McLuhan's article "Joyce, Mallarmé, and the Press" in *The Interior Landscape: The Literary Criticism of Marshall McLuhan*, selected, compiled and edited by Eugene McNamara.

"Seeing Things": The business about "photoreceptors" comes from the article "Seeing the natural world with a physicist's eye" in the *New York Times*, 2 November, 2010.

"Thank-you note after a morning visit": "Love stories depend on disappointment" is Jeffrey Eugenides' notion in his introduction to *My Mistress's Sparrow is Dead*.

"Yellow Leather Gloves": The Rilke lines are from the second of the *Duino Elegies*, trans. Stephen Mitchell.

The italicized line in "The Biographer" is from Thoreau's *Walden*.

The read-out line in "Letters" comes from e.e. cummings' "somewhere i have never travelled, gladly beyond."

When I wrote "The biographer addresses the railing," I was reading Lynne A. Isbell's book *The Fruit, The Tree, and the Serpent: Why we see so well*. A sentence from Montaigne's "That to philosophize is to learn to die" is echoed here.

"He was a beautiful man. What more needs to be said?": In Joseph O'Connor's novel *Ghost Light*, words similar to these are attributed to the early 20th-century Irish actress Molly Allgood. The poem refers, as well, to John Donne.

The epigraph to section two is quoted from Eamon Stanley's *The Aesthetic of the Everyday*.

"Larger Blue Flag: Irises" ends with a re-working of the last line in Ciaran Carson's poem "Soot."

"Rain, Summer" quotes Psalm 136:7.

In "Sojourn: biblical in the garden," the italicized sentence comes from 1 Peter 1:24.

"Haar: frost smoke off the North Atlantic" refers to the German folktale "The Dancing Fox."

Epigraph, section three: The lines from "At Innernytie" appear in John Glenday's *Grain*.

"Rope Handles": The science that closes the poem comes from a David Suzuki program, "Life and Death," CBC radio, 22 August, 2010. The three-word quotation is from Charles Lee O'Donnell's poem "Wonder."

"Bread" refers to Genesis I.

In "Reading Around" a sentence from Michael Cunningham's novel *By Nightfall* and a question and response from Steven Hayward's *Don't Be Afraid* are approximately quoted.

The italicized half-line in "Beatrice" is quoted from Dante's *The Inferno*, canto two, trans. Robert Pinsky.

"Natural History Museum" quotes Beatrix Potter's *The Tale of Johnny Town-mouse* and *The Tale of Mr Tod*. The line from the former is abbreviated. The epigraph is from a letter to her publisher, in which Potter quotes this Westmoreland ballad.

"Picture Books": *Alla Prima* is the technique of completing the picture surface in one session … and with such opacity that neither previous drawing nor underpainting – if these exist – modifies the final effect.

The italicized line in "Estate Library" appears in Colin McAdam's *Falling*.

"Shoreland": The expression "prosaic days" is Emily Dickinson's.

"Waste Places": The image of the imagination as a set of stairs is one that I heard Seamus Heaney use in a conversation with Eleanor Wachtel, CBC radio, 23 May 2010.

Acknowledgements

Arc: "Jacklight" and "Rain, Summer"

Malahat Review: "What the construction worker said," "Pictures," "A Visitor to the Garden, April," "Cab Ride, Paris," "Plovers," and "Footwork in Four Seasons"

Fiddlehead: "The Poet as Invalid," "Picture Books," "From London, by way of Montreal, March," "Larger Blue Flag: Irises," "Raspberries," "Heat Week," and "Signs"

Manchester Review: "Fire and Grammar," "*Haar*: frost smoke off the North Atlantic," and "Biography of the Poet"

Best Canadian Poetry in English, 2010: "Heat in April"

"Waste Places" first appeared in *A Crystal Through Which Light Passes: Glosas for Page*, edited by Jesse Ferguson, BuschekBooks.

My thanks to the anthology and journal editors who published these poems, sometimes in slightly different versions.

The New Brunswick Arts Board provided much-appreciated financial support during the writing of this book.

Richard Dionne, with his usual kindness, helped with the cover image and saw the book through press.

My warmest thanks to Evan Jones – best of editors – who patiently and persuasively commented on every poem, making a better book of my manuscript.